learn to do
tunisian
lace stitches

Tunisian crochet has a multi-national history, with early examples found in Africa and Central Asia. It was a popular technique in Victorian-era publications, with patterns using Tunisian Simple Stitch and cross-stitch embroidery on the finished fabric's grid being all the rage. Tunisian crochet was frequently referred to as "afghan stitch."

This is a beautiful and versatile stitch technique that borrows elements from both knitting and crochet, creating a pleasing fusion of the two techniques. Stitch possibilities include textured stitches, ribs, laces and many others.

The lace-stitch patterns used in this book are clever combinations of basic Tunisian crochet stitches by Tunisian crochet expert Kim Guzman. With a little practice, and Kim's beautiful patterns, you too can become a Tunisian crochet expert.

introduction

A Tunisian crochet hook is longer than a regular crochet hook. It has a hook at one end and a knob at the other end to hold the stitches on the hook. In Tunisian crochet, stitches are picked up and held on the hook for the first part of the row, and then worked off the hook for the second part of the row.

6 Information

25 Bobbles in Blue Throw

28 Rustic Table Runner

32 Bonny Waves Wrap

35 Peek-a-Boo Throw

37 Symphony Capelet

41 Carnival Market Bag

44 Starburst Cloche & Scarf

47 Rolled Collar Wrap

51 Swirls Baby Afghan

54 Opulent Shells Wrap

58 Stitch Guide

59 Metric Conversion Charts

contents

tunisian lace information

An understanding of the basic Tunisian crochet stitches is essential to the successful working of the Tunisian Lace Stitch patterns. Each Tunisian stitch has its own unique insertion point and method of drawing up the yarn. You will easily master these stitches once you understand the basics. Instructions for these basic Tunisian stitches can be found on pages 6–11.

What is Tunisian crochet and how is it different than regular crochet? Standard Tunisian crochet stitches are worked in an assembly line fashion, i.e. the stitch loops are held on the hook and then worked off. For the first part of the row, you pick up and hold loops on the hook as you work across the row; for the second part, you work those loops off the hook. The various Tunisian stitches are created by way of the yarn over, where the hook is inserted and how the loops are worked off the hook.

To accomplish Tunisian crochet, you will need a different kind of hook. A Tunisian crochet hook is longer than a regular crochet hook. It has a hook at one end and a knob at the other end to hold the stitches on the hook. Because Tunisian crochet hooks are available in various lengths (both straight and flexible), when trying to determine what length hook you need, select a hook that can hold a project that is up to three times longer than the hook.

A flexible hook can be used for wider or heavier projects. This type of hook has a crochet hook on one end and a flexible cable between the hook and the knob on the other end. The cable allows a large number of stitches to be held on the length of the hook.

STITCHES
BASIC FOUNDATION ROW
1. Work Loops On Hook (work lps on hook)

Ch as stated, sk first ch *(see Fig. 1A)*,

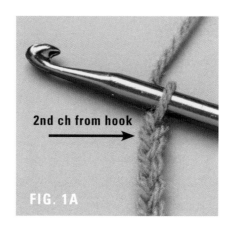

2nd ch from hook →

FIG. 1A

insert hook in 2nd ch from hook *(see Fig. 1B)*,

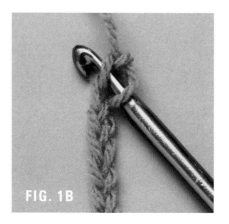

FIG. 1B

yo, pull lp through ch, holding all lps on hook (you will now have 2 lps on hook *(see Fig. 1C)*,

FIG. 1C

[insert hook in next ch, yo, pull lp through ch] across *(see Fig. 1D)*.

FIG. 1D

You will have the same number of lps on hook as number of chs in the Basic Foundation Row.

2. Standard Closing or Work Loops Off Hook (Standard Closing)

Ch 1 (see Fig. 2A),

FIG. 2A

[yo, pull through 2 lps on hook (see Fig. 2B)] across.

FIG. 2B

Last lp on hook is first lp of next row.
NOTE: *Typically to begin working lps off the hook in Tunisian most of our books will tell you to yo, pull through 1 lp, (yo and pull through 2 lps on hook) until all lps have been worked off the hook. However for this book and DVD designer Kim Guzman describes the first yo and pull through 1 lp, as a ch-1.*

TUNISIAN SIMPLE STITCH (TSS)

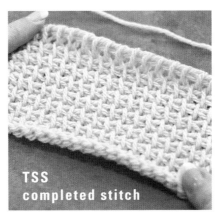

TSS completed stitch

Ch as stated, work **Basic Foundation Row** (see Figs. 1A–2B).
Sk first vertical bar, insert hook under front vertical bar from right to left (see Fig. 3A),

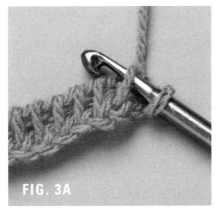

FIG. 3A

yo, pull up lp, (see Fig. 3B)

FIG. 3B

[insert hook under next vertical bar from right to left, yo, pull up lp] across. At end of row, work into ch-1 from previous row, insert hook under both front and back lps of ch-1 (see Fig. 3C),

FIG. 3C

yo and pull up lp. You should now have same number of loops on hook as starting ch.
Work lps off hook using **Standard Closing** (see Figs. 2A–2B). Last lp on hook is first lp of next row.

TUNISIAN REVERSE STITCH (TRS)

TRS
completed stitch

Ch as stated, work **Basic Foundation Row** (see Figs. 1A–2B).
Sk first vertical bar, keeping hook to back of work, insert hook from right to left (side to side) under back vertical bar (see Fig. 4A),

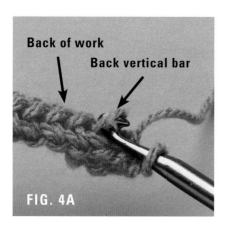

Back of work

Back vertical bar

FIG. 4A

yo, pull lp through (see Fig. 4B),

FIG. 4B

hold all lps on hook as you work across the row.
At end of row, work into ch-1 from previous row, insert hook under both front and back lps of ch-1 (see Fig. 3C), yo and pull up lp. You should now have same number of loops on hook as starting ch.
Work lps off hook using **Standard Closing** (see Figs. 2A–2B). Last lp on hook is first lp of next row.

TUNISIAN KNIT STITCH (TKS)

TKS
completed stitch

Ch as stated, work **Basic Foundation Row** (see Figs. 1A–2B).
Sk first vertical bar, insert hook from front to back (see Fig. 5A),

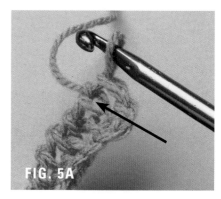

FIG. 5A

between front and back vertical bars (see Fig. 5B) of same st,

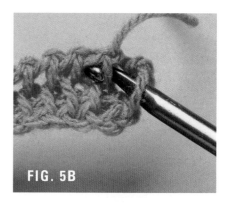

FIG. 5B

yo, pull lp through (see Fig. 5C),

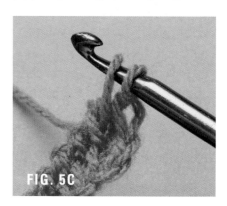

FIG. 5C

hold all lps on hook as you work across the row.

At end of row, work into ch-1 from previous row, insert hook under both front and back lps of ch-1 *(see Fig. 3C)*, yo and pull up lp. You should now have same number of loops on hook as starting ch.

Work lps off hook using **Standard Closing** *(see Figs. 2A–2B)*. Last lp on hook is first lp of next row.

MAKE ONE (M1)

M1
completed stitch

Insert hook in ch sp or as indicated, yo *(see Fig. 6A)*,

FIG. 6A

pull lp through *(see Fig. 6B)*,

FIG. 6B

hold all lps on hook.

TUNISIAN DOUBLE STITCH (TDS)

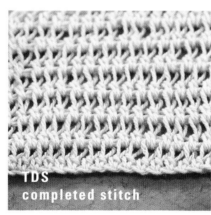

TDS
completed stitch

Note: *Insertion of hook shown here is as for knit stitch. This stitch can also be created using other insertion points if desired.*

Ch as stated, work **Basic Foundation Row** *(see Figs. 1A–2B)*.

Ch 2 at beginning of row, sk first vertical bar, yo, insert hook from front to back *(see Fig. 7A)*,

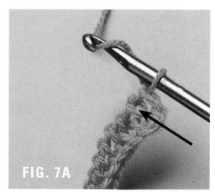

FIG. 7A

between front and back vertical bars *(see Fig. 7B)* of same st,

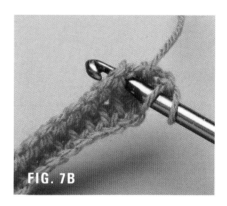

FIG. 7B

yo, pull lp through *(see Fig. 7C)*,

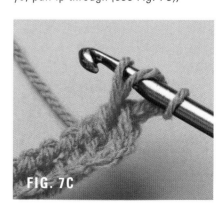

FIG. 7C

yo, pull through 2 lps on hook *(see Fig. 7D)*,

FIG. 7D

holding all lps on hook across your work.

At end of row, work into ch-1 from previous row, insert hook under both front and back lps of ch-1 *(see Fig. 3C)*, yo and pull up lp. You should now have same number of loops on hook as starting ch.

Work lps off hook using **Standard Closing** *(see Figs. 2A–2B)*. Last lp on hook is first lp of next row.

TUNISIAN TREBLE STITCH (TTRS)

TTRS
completed stitch

Note: *Insertion of hook shown here is as for knit stitch. This stitch can also be created using other insertion points if desired.*

Ch as stated, work **Basic Foundation Row** *(see Figs. 1A–2B)*.
Ch 2 at beginning of row, sk first vertical bar, yo twice, insert hook from front to back *(see Fig. 8A)*, between

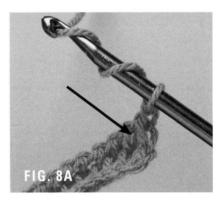
FIG. 8A

front and back vertical bars *(see Fig. 8B)* of same st,

FIG. 8B

yo, pull lp through *(see Fig. 8C)*,

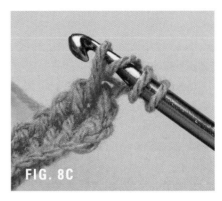
FIG. 8C

[yo, pull through 2 lps on hook *(see Fig. 8D)*]

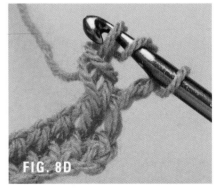
FIG. 8D

twice *(see Fig. 8E)*,

FIG. 8E

holding all lps on hook across your work.

At end of row, work into ch-1 from previous row, insert hook under both front and back lps of ch-1 (see Fig. 3C), yo and pull up lp. You should now have same number of loops on hook as starting ch.

Work lps off hook using **Standard Closing** (see Figs. 2A–2B). Last lp on hook is first lp of next row.

TUNISIAN EXTENDED STITCH (TES)

TES
completed stitch

Note: Insertion of hook shown here is as for knit stitch. This stitch can also be created using other insertion points if desired.

Ch as stated, work **Basic Foundation Row** (see Figs. 1A–2B).

Sk first vertical bar, insert hook from front to back (see Fig. 9A),

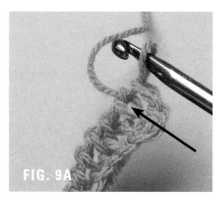

FIG. 9A

between front and back vertical bars (see Fig. 9B) of same st,

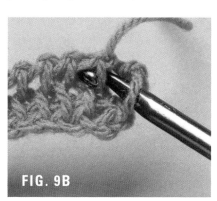

FIG. 9B

yo, pull lp through (see Fig. 9C),

FIG. 9C

ch 1 (see Fig. 9D),

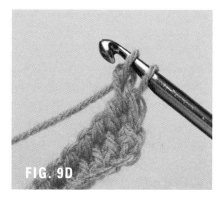

FIG. 9D

holding all lps on hook across your work.

At end of row, work into ch-1 from previous row, insert hook under both front and back lps of ch-1 (see Fig. 3C), yo and pull up lp. You should now have same number of loops on hook as starting ch.

Work lps off hook using **Standard Closing** (see Figs. 2A–2B). Last lp on hook is first lp of next row.

stitch pattern number 1

SPECIAL STITCHES

For step-by-step stitch information see Figs. 1–9 on pages 6–11.

Basic Foundation Row:

1. **Work Loops On Hook (work lps on hook):** Ch as stated, sk first ch, insert hook in 2nd ch from hook, yo, pull lp through ch, holding all lps on hook (you will now have 2 lps on hook), [insert hook in next ch, yo, pull lp through ch] across.

2. **Standard Closing or Work Loops Off Hook (Standard Closing):** Ch 1, [yo, pull through 2 lps on hook] across.

Tunisian Reverse Stitch (TRS): Keeping hook to back of work, insert hook from right to left (side to side) under back vertical bar, yo, pull lp through.

Tunisian Knit Stitch (TKS): Insert hook from front to back of work, between front and back vertical bars of same st, yo, pull lp through.

Tunisian Bobble: Yo, insert hook in horizontal bar above 3-st group, yo, pull lp through, yo, pull through 2 lps on hook, [yo, insert hook in same horizontal bar, yo, pull lp through, yo, pull through 2 lps on hook] twice, yo, pull through 3 lps on hook, ch 1.

Make One (M1): Insert hook in ch-1 sp, yo, pull lp through.

Tunisian Simple Stitch (TSS): Keeping hook to front of work, insert hook from right to left (side to side) under front vertical bar, yo, pull lp through.

INSTRUCTIONS

PATTERN NO. 1

Row 1: Basic Foundation Row (see Special Stitches)

1. Ch a multiple of 10 plus 7, **work lps on hook** (see Special Stitches);

2. **Standard Closing** (see Special Stitches). Last lp on hook counts as first st of next row.

Row 2:

1. Sk first vertical bar, **TRS** (see Special Stitches) across;

2. Ch 1, yo pull through 2 lps on hook, *ch 1, yo, pull through 4 lps on hook, ch 1, [yo, pull through 2 lps on hook] twice, rep from * across.

Row 3:

1. Sk first vertical bar, **TKS** (see Special Stitches), [**Tunisian Bobble** (see Special Stitches), 2 TKS] across;

2. Ch 1, yo, pull through 2 lps on hook, *ch 1, yo, pull through 2 lps on hook, ch 1, [yo, pull through 2 lps on hook] twice, rep from * across.

Row 4:

1. Sk first vertical bar, TKS, [**M1** (see Special Stitches), TKS, M1, 2 TKS] across;

2. Standard Closing.

Row 5:

1. Sk first vertical bar, TRS across;

2. Standard Closing.

Row 6:

1. Sk first vertical bar, [sk next vertical bar, **TSS** (see Special Stitches), TSS in last sk vertical bar] across;

2. Standard Closing.

Rep rows 2–6 for pattern. ●

stitch pattern number 2

SPECIAL STITCHES

For step-by-step stitch information see Figs. 1–9 on pages 6–11.

Basic Foundation Row:

1. Work Loops On Hook (work lps on hook): Ch as stated, sk first ch, insert hook in 2nd ch from hook, yo, pull lp through ch, holding all lps on hook (you will now have 2 lps on hook), [insert hook in next ch, yo, pull lp through ch] across.

2. Standard Closing or Work Loops Off Hook (Standard Closing): Ch 1, [yo, pull through 2 lps on hook] across.

Tunisian Knit Stitch (TKS): Insert hook from front to back of work, between front and back vertical bars of same st, yo, pull lp through.

Tunisian Reverse Stitch (TRS): Keeping hook to back of work, insert hook from right to left (side to side) under back vertical bar, yo, pull lp through.

INSTRUCTIONS

PATTERN NO. 2

Row 1: Basic Foundation Row (see Special Stitches)

1. Ch a multiple of 10 plus 6 (must be a minimum of 26 chs), **work lps on hook** (see Special Stitches);

2. Standard Closing (see Special Stitches). Last lp on hook counts as first st of next row.

Row 2:

1. Sk first vertical bar, **TRS** (see Special Stitches) across;

2. Standard Closing.

Row 3:

1. Ch 1, sk first vertical bar, *[yo, TRS] 5 times, 5 TRS, rep from * across to last 5 vertical bars, [yo, TRS] 5 times;

2. Ch 2, *[remove first lp from hook and drop yo from hook, replace first lp back on hook, yo, pull through 2 lps on hook] 5 times, [yo, pull through 2 lps on hook] 5 times, rep from * across to last 11 lps on hook, [remove next lp from hook, and drop yo from hook, replace lp back on hook, yo, pull through 2 lps on hook] 5 times.

Row 4:

1. Sk first vertical bar, TRS, [3 **TKS** (see Special Stitches), 7 TRS] across to last 4 vertical bars, 3 TKS, TRS in ch before last vertical bar;

2. Standard Closing.

Row 5: Rep row 2.

Row 6:

1. Sk first vertical bar, 5 TRS, *[yo, TRS] 5 times, 5 TRS, rep from * across;

2. Ch 1, *[yo, pull through 2 lps on hook] 5 times, [remove next lp from hook, drop yo from hook, replace lp back on hook, yo, pull through 2 lps on hook] 5 times, rep from * across to last 6 lps on hook, [yo, pull through 2 lps on hook] 5 times.

Row 7:

1. Sk first vertical bar, 6 TRS, [3 TKS, 7 TRS] across to last 9 vertical bars, 3 TKS, 6 TRS;

2. Standard Closing.

Rep rows 2–7 for pattern. ●

stitch pattern number 3

SPECIAL STITCHES

For step-by-step stitch information see Figs. 1–9 on pages 6–11.

Tunisian Knit Stitch (TKS): Insert hook from front to back of work, between front and back vertical bars of same st, yo, pull lp through.

Tunisian Double Stitch (TDS): Yo, insert hook as for **TKS** or as indicated, yo, pull lp through, yo, pull through 2 lps on hook.

Make One (M1): Insert hook in ch-1 sp, yo, pull lp through.

INSTRUCTIONS

PATTERN NO. 3

Row 1:

1. Ch a multiple of 6 plus 5 *(must be a minimum of 17 chs)*, sk first ch, holding all lps on hook, *[**TDS** *(see Special Stitches)* in next ch] 3 times, [insert hook in next ch, yo, pull lp through] 3 times, rep from * across to last 4 chs, [TDS in next ch] 3 times, insert hook in last ch, yo, pull lp through;

2. Ch 2, yo, pull through 4 lps on hook, ch 1, *[yo, pull through 2 lps on hook] 3 times, ch 1, yo, pull through 4 lps on hook, ch 1, rep from * across to last 2 lps on hook, yo, pull through both lps on hook. Last lp on hook counts as first st of next row.

Row 2:

1. Sk first vertical bar, **M1** *(see Special Stitches)*, sk next 3-st group, M1, [3 **TKS** *(see Special Stitches)*, M1, sk next 3-st group, M1] across to last vertical bar, TKS in ch before last vertical bar;

2. Ch 1, yo, pull through 2 lps on hook, ch 1, *[yo, pull though 2 lps on hook] 5 times, ch 1, rep from * across to last 3 lps on hook, [yo, pull through 2 lps on hook] twice.

Row 3:

1. Sk first vertical bar, [TKS, M1, TKS, 3 TDS] across to last 3 vertical bars, TKS, M1, 2 TKS;

2. Ch 1, [yo, pull through 2 lps on hook] 3 times, *ch 1, yo, pull through 4 lps on hook, ch 1, [yo, pull through 2 lps on hook] 3 times, rep from * across to last 2 lps on hook, yo, pull through both lps on hook.

Row 4:

1. Sk first vertical bar, [3 TKS, M1, sk next 3-st group, M1] across to last 4 vertical bars, 4 TKS;

2. Ch 1, [yo, pull through 2 lps on hook] 4 times, *ch 1, [yo, pull through 2 lps on hook] 5 times, rep from * across.

Row 5:

1. Sk first vertical bar, [3 TDS, TKS, M1, TKS] across to last 4 vertical bars, 3 TDS, TKS;

2. Ch 2, yo, pull through 4 lps on hook, ch 1, *[yo, pull through 2 lps on hook] 3 times, ch 1, yo, pull through 4 lps on hook, ch 1, rep from * across to last 2 lps on hook, yo, pull through both lps on hook.

Rep rows 2–5 for pattern. ●

stitch pattern number 4

SPECIAL STITCHES

For step-by-step stitch information see Figs. 1–9 on pages 6–11.

Basic Foundation Row:

Standard Closing or Work Loops Off Hook (Standard Closing):
Ch 1, [yo, pull through 2 lps on hook] across.

Tunisian Treble Stitch (TTRS): Yo twice, insert hook as for **TKS** or as indicated yo, pull lp through, [yo, pull through 2 lps on hook] twice.

Tunisian Knit Stitch (TKS): Insert hook from front to back of work, between front and back vertical bars of same st, yo, pull lp through.

Tunisian Double Stitch (TDS): Yo, insert hook as for **TKS** or as indicated, yo, pull lp through, yo, pull through 2 lps on hook.

Tunisian Cluster (TCL): Yo twice, insert hook as for **TSS** under 2 front vertical bars at same time, yo, pull lp through, [yo, pull through 2 lps on hook] twice, yo twice, insert hook under same 2 front vertical bars, yo, pull lp through, [yo, pull through 2 lps on hook] 3 times.

INSTRUCTIONS

PATTERN NO. 4

Row 1:

1. Ch a multiple of 2 plus 1 *(must be a minimum of 5 chs)*, holding all lps on hook, **TDS** *(see Special Stitches)* in 3rd ch from hook and in each ch across;

2. Standard Closing of Basic Foundation Row *(see Special Stitches)*.

Row 2:

1. Ch 3, sk first vertical bar, **TCL** *(see Special Stitches)* across to last vertical bar, **TTRS** *(see Special Stitches)* in last vertical bar;

2. [Ch 1, yo, pull through 2 lps on hook] across. **Note:** *This is not a Standard Closing.*

Row 3:

1. Ch 2, sk first vertical bar, [TDS by inserting hook under horizontal strand before TCL and ch-1 sp at same time, TDS in TCL] across to last vertical bar *(see Fig. A)*, TDS in top of TTRS;

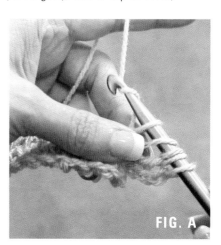

FIG. A

2. Standard Closing.

Rep rows 2 and 3 for pattern. •

stitch pattern number 5

SPECIAL STITCHES

For step-by-step stitch information see Figs. 1–9 on pages 6–11.

Basic Foundation Row:

1. **Work Loops On Hook (work lps on hook):** Ch as stated, sk first ch, insert hook in 2nd ch from hook, yo, pull lp through ch, holding all lps on hook (you will now have 2 lps on hook), [insert hook in next ch, yo, pull lp through ch] across.

2. **Standard Closing or Work Loops Off Hook (Standard Closing):** Ch 1, [yo, pull through 2 lps on hook] across.

Tunisian Knit Stitch (TKS): Insert hook from front to back of work, between front and back vertical bars of same st, yo, pull lp through.

Tunisian Reverse Stitch (TRS): Keeping hook to back of work, insert hook from right to left (side to side) under back vertical bar, yo, pull lp through.

Tunisian Double Stitch (TDS): Yo, insert hook as for **TKS** or as indicated, yo, pull lp through, yo, pull through 2 lps on hook.

INSTRUCTIONS

PATTERN NO. 5

Row 1: Basic Foundation Row (see Special Stitches)

1. Ch a multiple of 3 plus 2, **work lps on hook** (see Special Stitches);

2. [Ch 2, yo, pull through 4 lps on hook] across to last 2 lps on hook, ch 1, yo, pull through both lps on hook. Last lp on hook counts as first st of next row.

Row 2:

1. Sk first vertical bar, [3 **TDS** (see Special Stitches) in horizontal bar above 3-st group] across to last vertical bar, **TKS** (see Special Stitches);

2. **Standard Closing of Basic Foundation Row** (see Special Stitches).

Row 3:

1. Sk first vertical bar, **TRS** (see Special Stitches) across to last vertical bar, TRS in ch before last vertical bar;

2. [Ch 2, yo, pull through 4 lps on hook] across to last 2 lps on hook, ch 1, yo, pull through both lps on hook.

Rep rows 2 and 3 for pattern. ●

stitch pattern number 6

SPECIAL STITCHES

For step-by-step stitch information see Figs. 1–9 on pages 6–11.

Tunisian Knit Stitch (TKS): Insert hook from front to back of work, between front and back vertical bars of same st, yo, pull lp through.

Make One (M1): Insert hook in ch-1 sp, yo, pull lp through.

Tunisian Extended Stitch (TES): Insert hook from front to back, between front and back vertical bars of same st, yo, pull lp through, ch 1.

INSTRUCTIONS

PATTERN NO. 6

Row 1:

1. Ch a multiple of 6 plus 3 *(must be a minimum of 15 chs)*, holding all lps on hook, [insert hook in next ch, yo, pull lp through] twice, *[insert hook in next ch, yo, pull lp through, ch 1] 3 times, [insert hook in next ch, yo, pull lp through] 3 times, rep from * across;

2. Ch 1, [yo, pull through 2 lps on hook] twice, *ch 1, yo, pull through 4 lps on hook, ch 1, [yo, pull through 2 lps on hook] 3 times, rep from * across. Last lp on hook counts as first st of next row.

Row 2:

1. Sk first vertical bar, 2 **TKS** *(see Special Stitches)*, [insert hook in horizontal bar above 3-st group, yo, pull lp through, 3 TKS] across;

2. Ch 1, [yo, pull through 2 lps on hook] twice, *ch 1, yo, pull through 2 lps on hook, ch 1, [yo, pull through 2 lps on hook] 3 times, rep from * across.

Row 3:

1. Sk first vertical bar, 2 TKS, [**M1** *(see Special Stitches)*, ch 1, **TES** *(see Special Stitches)*, M1, ch 1, 3 TKS] across;

2. Ch 1, [yo, pull through 2 lps on hook] twice, *ch 1, yo, pull through 4 lps on hook, ch 1, [yo, pull through 2 lps on hook] 3 times, rep from * across.

Rep rows 2 and 3 for pattern. •

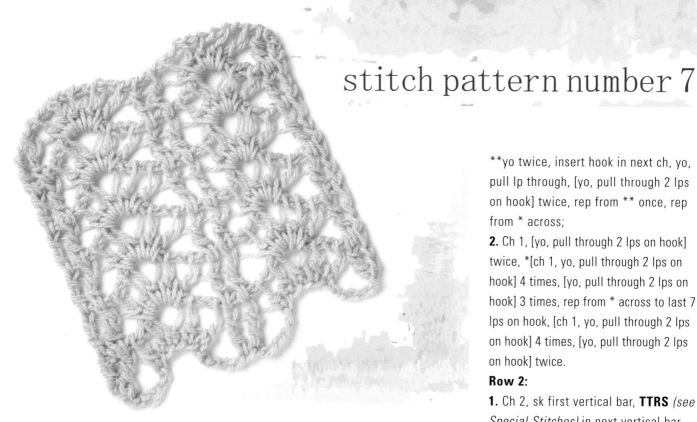

SPECIAL STITCHES

For step-by-step stitch information see Figs. 1–9 on pages 6–11.

Tunisian Treble Stitch (TTRS): Yo twice, insert hook as for **TKS** or as indicated, yo, pull lp through, [yo, pull through 2 lps on hook] twice.

Tunisian Double Stitch (TDS): Yo, insert hook as for **TKS** or as indicated, yo, pull lp through, yo, pull through 2 lps on hook.

INSTRUCTIONS

PATTERN NO. 7

Row 1:

1. Ch a multiple of 15 plus 3 *(must be a minimum of 33 chs)*, holding all lps on hook, yo twice, insert hook in 3rd ch from hook, yo, pull lp through, [yo, pull through 2 lps on hook] twice, *sk next 4 chs, [yo, insert hook in next ch, yo, pull lp through, yo, pull through 2 lps on hook] 5 times, sk next 4 chs,

**yo twice, insert hook in next ch, yo, pull lp through, [yo, pull through 2 lps on hook] twice, rep from ** once, rep from * across;

2. Ch 1, [yo, pull through 2 lps on hook] twice, *[ch 1, yo, pull through 2 lps on hook] 4 times, [yo, pull through 2 lps on hook] 3 times, rep from * across to last 7 lps on hook, [ch 1, yo, pull through 2 lps on hook] 4 times, [yo, pull through 2 lps on hook] twice.

Row 2:

1. Ch 2, sk first vertical bar, **TTRS** *(see Special Stitches)* in next vertical bar, *5 **TDS** *(see Special Stitches)* in 3rd st of next 5-TDS group, TTRS in each of next 2 TTRS, rep from * across;

2. Ch 1, [yo, pull through 2 lps on hook] twice, *[ch 1, yo, pull through 2 lps on hook] 4 times, [yo, pull through 2 lps on hook] 3 times, rep from * across to last 7 lps on hook, [ch 1, yo, pull through 2 lps on hook] 4 times, [yo, pull through 2 lps on hook] twice.

Rep row 2 for pattern. ●

stitch pattern number 8

SPECIAL STITCHES

For step-by-step stitch information see Figs. 1–9 on pages 6–11.

Basic Foundation Row:

Standard Closing or Work Loops Off Hook (Standard Closing):
Ch 1, [yo, pull through 2 lps on hook] across.

Tunisian Knit Stitch (TKS): Insert hook from front to back of work, between front and back vertical bars of same st, yo, pull lp through.

Tunisian Double Stitch (TDS): Yo, insert hook as for **TKS** or as indicated, yo, pull lp through, yo, pull through 2 lps on hook.

INSTRUCTIONS

PATTERN NO. 8

Row 1:

1. Ch a multiple of 10 plus 8 *(must be a minimum of 28 chs)*, holding all lps on hook, sk next 2 chs, *[yo, insert hook in next ch, yo, pull lp through, yo, pull through 2 lps on hook] 5 times, [insert hook in next ch, yo, pull lp through] 5 times, rep from * across to last 6 chs, [yo, insert hook in next ch, yo, pull lp through, yo, pull through 2 lps on hook] 5 times, insert hook in last ch, yo, pull lp through;

2. Ch 3, *yo, pull through 6 lps on hook, ch 2, [yo, pull through 2 lps on hook] 5 times, ch 2, rep from * across to last 7 lps on hook, yo, pull through 6 lps on hook, ch 2, yo, pull through last 2 lps on hook. Last lp on hook counts as first st of next row.

Row 2:

1. Sk first vertical bar, [5 **TDS** *(see Special Stitches)* in horizontal bar above 5-st group, 5 **TKS** *(see Special Stitches)*] across to horizontal bar above last 5-st group, 5 TDS in last horizontal bar, TKS in ch before last vertical bar;

2. Standard Closing of Basic Foundation Row *(see Special Stitches)*.

Row 3:

1. Sk first vertical bar, [5 TKS, 5 TDS as for TKS] across to last 6 vertical bars, 6 TKS;

2. Ch 1, *[yo, pull through 2 lps on hook] 5 times, ch 2, yo, pull through 6 lps on hook, ch 2, rep from * across to last 7 lps on hook, [yo, pull through 2 lps on hook] 6 times.

Row 4:

1. Sk first vertical bar, [5 TKS, 5 TDS in horizontal bar above 5-st group] across to last 6 vertical bars, 6 TKS;

2. Standard Closing.

Row 5:

1. Sk first vertical bar, [5 TDS, 5 TKS] across to last 6 vertical bars, 5 TDS, TKS;

2. Ch 3, *yo, pull through 6 lps on hook, ch 2, [yo, pull through 2 lps on hook] 5 times, ch 2, rep from * across to last 7 lps on hook, yo, pull through 6 lps on hook, ch 2, yo, pull through last 2 lps on hook. Rep rows 2–5 for pattern. ●

stitch pattern number 9

SPECIAL STITCHES

For step-by-step stitch information see Figs. 1–9 on pages 6–11.

Basic Foundation Row:

1. **Work Loops On Hook (work lps on hook):** Ch as stated, sk first ch, insert hook in 2nd ch from hook, yo, pull lp through ch, holding all lps on hook (you will now have 2 lps on hook), [insert hook in next ch, yo, pull lp through ch] across.

2. **Standard Closing or Work Loops Off Hook (Standard Closing):** Ch 1, [yo, pull through 2 lps on hook] across.

Make one (M1): Insert hook in ch-1 sp, yo, pull lp through.

Tunisian Double Stitch (TDS): Yo, insert hook as for **TSS** or as indicated, yo, pull lp through, yo, pull through 2 lps on hook.

Tunisian Simple Stitch (TSS): Keeping hook to front of work, insert hook from right to left (side to side) under front vertical bar, yo, pull lp through.

Tunisian Knit Stitch (TKS): Insert hook from front to back of work, between front and back vertical bars of same st, yo, pull lp through.

INSTRUCTIONS

PATTERN NO. 9

Row 1: Basic Foundation Row *(see Special Stitches)*

1. Ch a multiple of 3 plus 2 *(must be a minimum of 8 chs)*, **work lps on hook** *(see Special Stitches)*;

2. **Standard Closing** *(see Special Stitches)*.

Row 2:

1. Ch 1, sk first 3 vertical bars, **TDS** *(see Special Stitches)* in next vertical bar, working in front of last TDS, TDS in 2nd sk vertical bar, [sk next 2 vertical bars, TDS in next vertical bar, TDS in first sk vertical bar] across to last vertical bar, TDS in last vertical bar;

2. Ch 1, [yo, pull through 2 lps on hook, ch 1, yo, pull through 2 lps on hook] across to last 2 lps on hook, yo, pull through both lps on hook.

Row 3:

1. Sk first vertical bar, [**TSS** *(see Special Stitches)*, **M1** *(see Special Stitches)*, TSS] across to last vertical bar, **TKS** *(see Special Stitches)* in last vertical bar;

2. Standard Closing.

Rep rows 2 and 3 for pattern. ●

stitch pattern number 10

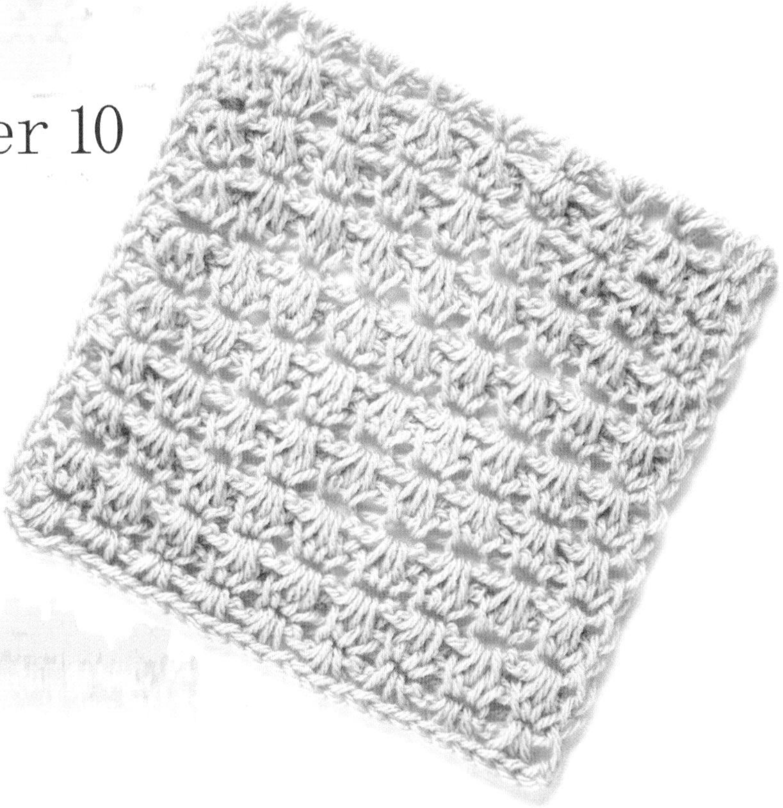

SPECIAL STITCHES

For step-by-step stitch information see Figs. 1–9 on pages 6–11.

Basic Foundation Row:

1. **Work Loops On Hook (work lps on hook):** Ch as stated, sk first ch, insert hook in 2nd ch from hook, yo, pull lp through ch, holding all lps on hook (you will now have 2 lps on hook), [insert hook in next ch, yo, pull lp through ch] across.

2. **Standard Closing or Work Loops Off Hook (Standard Closing):** Ch 1, [yo, pull through 2 lps on hook] across.

Tunisian Knit Stitch (TKS): Insert hook from front to back of work, between front and back vertical bars of same st, yo, pull lp through.

INSTRUCTIONS

PATTERN NO. 10

Row 1: Basic Foundation Row *(see Special Stitches)*

1. Ch a multiple of 3 plus 2 *(must be a minimum of 8 chs)*, **work lps on hook** *(see Special Stitches)*;

2. [Ch 2, yo, pull through 4 lps on hook] across to last 2 lps on hook, ch 1, yo, pull through both lps on hook. Last lp on hook counts as first st of next row.

Row 2:

1. Sk first vertical bar, insert hook in horizontal bar above next 3-st group, yo, pull lp through, yo, insert hook in same horizontal bar, yo, pull lp through, [insert hook in horizontal bar above next 3-st group, yo, pull lp through, yo, insert hook in same horizontal bar, yo, pull lp through] across to last vertical bar, **TKS** *(see Special Stitches)* in last vertical bar;

2. **Standard Closing** *(see Special Stitches)*.

Row 3:

1. Sk first vertical bar, TKS across;

2. [Ch 2, yo, pull through 4 lps on hook] across to last 2 lps on hook, ch 1, yo, pull through both lps on hook.

Rep rows 2 and 3 for pattern. ●

projects

Now that you've learned 10 unique lace stitch patterns, Kim Guzman is proud to present 10 of her favorite Tunisian crochet patterns.

- ❖ Bobbles in Blue Throw
- ❖ Rustic Table Runner
- ❖ Bonny Waves Wrap
- ❖ Peek-a-Boo Throw
- ❖ Symphony Capelet
- ❖ Carnival Market Bag
- ❖ Starburst Cloche & Scarf
- ❖ Rolled Collar Wrap
- ❖ Swirls Baby Afghan
- ❖ Opulent Shells Wrap

bobbles
in blue throw

bobbles in blue throw

SKILL LEVEL

INTERMEDIATE

FINISHED SIZE

49 x 56 inches

MATERIALS

- Red Heart Sport light (light worsted) weight yarn (2½ oz/165 yds/70g per skein):

   14 skeins #816 wedgewood blue
- Size G/6/4mm crochet hook
- Size K/10½/6.5mm afghan hook or size needed to obtain gauge

GAUGE

Size K hook: 9 sts = 2½ inches; 11 pattern rows = 4¾ inches

PATTERN NOTES

This item uses Stitch Pattern No. 1.
Chain-3 at beginning of row or round counts as first double crochet unless otherwise stated.
Join with slip stitch as indicated unless otherwise stated.

SPECIAL STITCHES

For step-by-step stitch information see Figs. 1–9 on pages 6–11.
Basic Foundation Row:
1. Work Loops On Hook (work lps on hook): Ch as stated, sk first ch, insert hook in 2nd ch from hook, yo, pull lp through ch, holding all lps on hook (you will now have 2 lps on hook), [insert hook in next ch, yo, pull lp through ch] across.

2. Standard Closing or Work Loops Off Hook (Standard Closing): Ch 1, [yo, pull through 2 lps on hook] across.
Tunisian Reverse Stitch (TRS): Keeping hook to back of work, insert hook from right to left (side to side) under back vertical bar, yo, pull lp through.
Tunisian Knit Stitch (TKS): Insert hook from front to back of work, between front and back vertical bars of same st, yo, pull lp through.
Tunisian Bobble: Yo, insert hook in horizontal bar above 3-st group, yo, pull lp through, yo, pull through 2 lps on hook, [yo, insert hook in same horizontal bar, yo, pull lp through, yo, pull through 2 lps on hook] twice, yo, pull through 3 lps on hook, ch 1.
Make One (M1): Insert hook in ch-1 sp, yo, pull lp through.
Tunisian Simple Stitch (TSS): Keeping hook to front of work, insert hook from right to left (side to side) under front vertical bar, yo, pull lp through.
V-stitch (V-st): (Dc, ch 1, dc) in place indicated.
Shell: (Dc, {ch 1, dc} twice) in place indicated.
Popcorn (pc): 3 dc in place indicated, drop lp from hook, insert hook in first dc of group, pull dropped lp through.

INSTRUCTIONS

THROW

Row 1: Basic Foundation Row (see Special Stitches)

1. With size K hook, ch 147, **work lps on hook** (see Special Stitches);
2. Standard Closing (see Special Stitches). Last lp on hook counts as first st of next row.
Row 2:
1. Sk first vertical bar, **TRS** (see Special Stitches) across;
2. Ch 1, yo pull through 2 lps on hook, *ch 1, yo, pull through 4 lps on hook, ch 1, [yo, pull through 2 lps on hook] twice, rep from * across.
Row 3:
1. Sk first vertical bar, **TKS** (see Special Stitches), [**Tunisian Bobble** (see Special Stitches), 2 TKS] across;
2. Ch 1, yo, pull through 2 lps on hook, *ch 1, yo, pull through 2 lps on hook, ch 1, [yo, pull through 2 lps on hook] twice, rep from * across.
Row 4:
1. Sk first vertical bar, TKS, [**M1** (see Special Stitches), TKS, M1, 2 TKS] across;
2. Standard Closing.
Row 5:
1. Sk first vertical bar, TRS across;
2. Standard Closing.
Row 6:
1. Sk first vertical bar, [sk next vertical bar, **TSS** (see Special Stitches), TSS in last sk vertical bar] across;
2. Standard Closing.
Rows 7–116: [Rep rows 2–6 consecutively] 22 times.
Rows 117–119: Rep rows 2–4.
Row 120: Working as for TRS, sk first vertical bar, sl st in each vertical bar across. Fasten off.

TRIM

Rnd 1: Working across short edge, with size G hook, **join** *(see Pattern Notes)* in first st, **ch 3** *(see Pattern Notes)*, evenly sp 143 dc across, (dc, ch 3, dc) in corner, evenly sp 159 dc in ends of rows across, (dc, ch 3, dc) in corner, working in starting ch on opposite side of row 1, evenly sp 143 dc across, (dc, ch 3, dc) in corner, evenly sp 159 dc in ends of rows across, dc in same st as beg ch-3, join with hdc in 3rd ch of beg ch-3, forming ch sp. *(4 ch-3 sps, 612 dc)*

Rnd 2: Ch 6 *(counts as first dc and ch-3)*, dc in ch sp just formed, *ch 1, dc in next st, [ch 1, sk next st, dc in next st] across to corner ch sp**, ch 1, (dc, ch 3, dc) in corner ch sp, rep from * around, ending last rep at **, ch 1, join in 3rd ch of beg ch-6.

Rnd 3: Ch 1, (sc, {ch 2, sc} 3 times) in first ch sp, *[ch 2, sc in next ch sp] across to next corner ch sp, ch 2**, (sc, {ch 2, sc} 3 times) in corner ch sp, rep from * around, ending last rep at **, join in beg sc.

Rnd 4: Sl st in first ch sp, ch 4 *(counts as first dc and ch-1)* dc in same ch sp, **shell** *(see Special Stitches)* in next ch sp, **V-st** *(see Special Stitches)* in next ch sp, *[ch 2, sk next ch sp, sc in next ch sp, ch 2, sk next ch sp, shell in next ch sp] across to last 2 ch sps before 5 corner ch sps, ch 2, sk next ch sp, sc in next ch sp, ch 2, sk next ch sp**, V-st in next ch sp, shell in next ch sp, V-st in next ch sp, rep from * around, ending last rep at **, join in 3rd ch of beg ch-4.

Rnd 5: Sl st in first ch sp, ch 1, sc in same ch sp, [ch 3, sc in next ch-1 sp] 3 times, work following steps to complete rnd:

A. *Ch 3, sk next ch-2 sp, **pc** *(see Special Stitches)* in next sc, ch 3, sk next ch-2 sp, sc in first ch-1 sp of next shell, ch 3, sc in next ch-1 sp of same shell, rep from * across to last sc before next corner;

B. Ch 3, sk next ch-2 sp, pc in next sc, ch 3, sk next ch-2 sp, sc in next ch-1 sp, [ch 3, sc in next ch-1 sp] 3 times;

C. [Rep steps A and B alternately] twice, rep step A;

D. Ch 3, sk next ch-2 sp, pc in next sc, ch 3, join in beg sc. Fasten off. •

rustic

SKILL LEVEL

INTERMEDIATE

FINISHED SIZE

12 x 50 inches

MATERIALS

- Red Heart Designer Sport light (light worsted) weight yarn (3 oz/279 yds/85g per skein):
    - 2 skeins #3261 terra cotta
    - 2 yds contrasting color
- Size G/6/4mm crochet hook
- Size K/10½/6.5mm afghan hook or size needed to obtain gauge

GAUGE

Size K hook: 7 sts = 2 inches; 9 pattern rows = 4 inches

PATTERN NOTES

This item uses Stitch Pattern No. 3. Runner is made beginning at the center, working in one direction, with a provisional cast-on *(see page 31)* and picking up stitches to work in opposite direction.

Join with slip stitch as indicated unless otherwise stated.

SPECIAL STITCHES

For step-by-step stitch information see Figs. 1–9 on pages 6–11.

Basic Foundation Row:

Standard Closing or Work Loops Off Hook (Standard Closing): Ch 1, [yo, pull through 2 lps on hook] across.

Tunisian Knit Stitch (TKS): Insert hook from front to back of work, between front and back vertical bars of same st, yo, pull lp through.

Tunisian Double Stitch (TDS): Yo, insert hook as for **TKS** or as indicated, yo, pull lp through, yo, pull through 2 lps on hook.

Make One (M1): Insert hook in ch-1 sp, yo, pull lp through.

Tunisian Knit Stitch decrease (TKS dec): Insert hook as for TKS through 2 vertical bars at same time, yo, pull lp through.

INSTRUCTIONS

RUNNER
FIRST SIDE
Row 1:

1. With size K hook, working provisional cast-on with contrasting color, ch 39, fasten off, working in **back bar of ch** *(see Fig. 1)*, **join** *(see Pattern Notes)* terra cotta in 3rd ch, holding all lps on hook, [insert hook in next ch, yo, pull lp through] 34 times, leaving rem chs unworked *(35 lps on hook)*;

Fig. 1
Back Bar of Chain

2. Standard Closing of Basic Foundation Row *(see Special Stitches)*. Last lp on hook counts as first st of next row.

Row 2:

1. Sk first vertical bar, [3 **TDS** *(see Special Stitches)*, 3 **TKS** *(see Special Stitches)*] across to last 4 vertical bars, 3 TDS, TKS;

2. Ch 2, yo, pull through 4 lps on hook, ch 1, *[yo, pull through 2 lps on hook] 3 times, ch 1, yo, pull through 4 lps on hook, ch 1, rep from * across to last 2 lps on hook, yo, pull through both lps on hook.

Row 3:

1. Sk first vertical bar, **M1** *(see Special Stitches)*, sk next 3-st group, M1, [3 TKS, M1, sk next 3-st group, M1] across to last vertical bar, TKS in ch before last vertical bar *(29 lps on hook)*;

2. Ch 1, yo, pull through 2 lps on hook, ch 1, *[yo, pull through 2 lps on hook]

5 times, ch 1, rep from * across to last 3 lps on hook, [yo, pull through 2 lps on hook] twice.

Row 4:
1. Sk first vertical bar, [TKS, M1, TKS, 3 TDS] across to last 3 vertical bars, TKS, M1, 2 TKS *(35 lps on hook)*;
2. Ch 1, [yo, pull through 2 lps on hook] 3 times, *ch 1, yo, pull through 4 lps on hook, ch 1, [yo, pull through 2 lps on hook] 3 times, rep from * across to last 2 lps on hook, yo, pull through both lps on hook.

Row 5:
1. Sk first vertical bar, [3 TKS, M1, sk next 3-st group, M1] across to last 4 vertical bars, 4 TKS *(30 lps on hook)*;
2. Ch 1, [yo, pull through 2 lps on hook] 4 times, *ch 1, [yo, pull through 2 lps on hook] 5 times, rep from * across.

Row 6:
1. Sk first vertical bar, [3 TDS, TKS, M1, TKS] across to last 4 vertical bars, 3 TDS, TKS *(35 lps on hook)*;
2. Ch 2 yo, pull through 4 lps on hook, ch 1, *[yo, pull through 2 lps on hook] 3 times, ch 1, yo, pull through 4 lps on hook, ch 1, rep from * across to last 2 lps on hook, yo, pull through both lps on hook.

Rows 7–50: [Rep rows 3–6 consecutively] 11 times.

Row 51:
1. Sk first vertical bar, M1, sk next 3-st group, M1, [3 TKS, M1, sk next 3-st group, M1] across to last vertical

bar, TKS in ch before last vertical bar *(29 lps on hook)*;
2. Standard Closing.

Row 52:
1. Sk first vertical bar, [3 TKS, 3 TDS] across to last 4 vertical bars, 4 TKS;
2. Ch 1, [yo, pull through 2 lps on hook] 3 times, *ch 1, yo, pull through 4 lps on hook, ch 1, [yo, pull through 2 lps on hook] 3 times, rep from * across to last 2 lps on hook, yo, pull through both lps on hook.

Row 53:
1. Sk first vertical bar, [3 TKS, M1, sk next 3-st group, M1] across to last 4 vertical bars, 4 TKS *(25 lps on hook)*;
2. Standard Closing.

Row 54:
1. Sk first vertical bar, **TKS dec** *(see Special Stitches)*, TKS across to last 2 vertical bars, TKS dec;
2. Standard Closing. Fasten off.

2ND SIDE
Row 1:
1. With RS facing and size K hook, working in vertical bars of row 1 of First Side, pull out provisional ch slowly *(see Fig. A)* and place lps on hook *(see Fig. B) (35 lps on hook)*;
2. Standard Closing.

Rows 2–53: Rep rows 2–53 of First Side.

Row 54:
1. Sk first vertical bar, TKS dec, TKS across to last 2 vertical bars, TKS dec;
2. Standard Closing. **Do not fasten off**.

FIG. A

FIG. B

TRIM
Rnd 1: Now working in rnds around outer edge in ends of rows and in sts, with size G hook, sk first vertical bar, ch 1, working as for TKS, sc in each vertical bar across, evenly sp sc in ends of rows down long edge, working as for TKS, sc in each vertical bar across, evenly sp sc in ends of rows up long edge, join in beg sc.
Rnd 2: Ch 3 *(counts as first dc)*, dc in each st around, join in 3rd ch of beg ch-3. Fasten off. ●

SKILL LEVEL

INTERMEDIATE

FINISHED SIZE

15 x 64 inches

MATERIALS

- NaturallyCaron.com Country medium (worsted) weight yarn (3 oz/185 yds/85g per ball):
    6 balls #0020 loden forest
- Sizes H/8/5mm and K/10½/6.5mm afghan hooks or size needed to obtain gauge

GAUGE

Size K hook: 11 TDS = 3 inches; unblocked

PATTERN NOTE

This item uses Stitch Pattern No. 8.

SPECIAL STITCHES

For step-by-step stitch information see Figs. 1–9 on pages 6–11.

Basic Foundation Row:

Standard Closing or Work Loops Off Hook (Standard Closing): Ch 1, [yo, pull through 2 lps on hook] across.

Tunisian Knit Stitch (TKS): Insert hook from front to back of work, between front and back vertical bars of same st, yo, pull lp through.

Tunisian Double Stitch (TDS): Yo, insert hook as for **TKS** or as indicated, yo, pull lp through, yo, pull through 2 lps on hook.

bonny waves

INSTRUCTIONS

WRAP

Row 1:

1. With size K hook, ch 58, holding all lps on hook, sk next 2 chs, *[yo, insert hook in next ch, yo, pull lp through, yo, pull through 2 lps on hook] 5 times, [insert hook in next ch, yo, pull lp through] 5 times, rep from * across to last 6 chs, [yo, insert hook in next ch, yo, pull lp through, yo, pull through 2 lps on hook] 5 times, insert hook in last ch, yo, pull lp through *(57 lps on hook)*;

2. Ch 3, *yo, pull through 6 lps on hook, ch 2, [yo, pull through 2 lps on hook] 5 times, ch 2, rep from * across to last 7 lps on hook, yo, pull through 6 lps on hook, ch 2, yo, pull through last 2 lps on hook. Last lp on hook counts as first st of next row.

Row 2:

1. Sk first vertical bar, [5 **TDS** *(see Special Stitches)* in horizontal bar above 5-st group, 5 **TKS** *(see Special Stitches)*] across to last 5-st group, 5 TDS in horizontal bar above last group, TKS in ch before last vertical bar;

2. Standard Closing of Basic Foundation Row *(see Special Stitches).*

Row 3:

1. Sk first vertical bar, [5 TKS, 5 TDS as for TKS] across to last 6 vertical bars, 6 TKS;

2. Ch 1, *[yo, pull through 2 lps on hook] 5 times, ch 2, yo, pull through 6 lps on hook, ch 2, rep from * across to last 7 lps on hook, [yo, pull through 2 lps on hook] 6 times.

Row 4:

1. Sk first vertical bar, [5 TKS, 5 TDS in horizontal bar above 5-st group] across to last 6 vertical bars, 6 TKS;

2. Standard Closing.

Row 5:

1. Sk first vertical bar, [5 TDS as for TKS, 5 TKS] across to last 6 vertical bars, 5 TDS as for TKS, TKS;

2. Ch 3, *yo, pull through 6 lps on hook, ch 2, [yo, pull through 2 lps on hook] 5 times, ch 2, rep from * across to last 7 lps on hook, yo, pull through 6 lps on hook, ch 2, yo, pull through last 2 lps on hook.

Rows 6–13: [Rep rows 2–5 consecutively] twice.

Rows 14 & 15: Rep rows 2 and 3.

Rows 16–28:

1. With size H hook, sk first vertical bar, TKS across *(57 lps on hook)*;

2. Standard Closing.

Rows 29–136: [Rep rows 2–28 consecutively] 4 times.

Rows 137–149: Rep rows 2–14.

Row 150: Sk first vertical bar, [sl st in each of next 5 vertical bars as for TKS, dc in each of next 5 vertical bars as for TKS] across to last 6 vertical bars, sl st in each of last 6 vertical bars as for TKS. Fasten off. ●

wrap

peek-a-boo throw

SKILL LEVEL

INTERMEDIATE

FINISHED SIZE

53½ inches square

MATERIALS

- Red Heart Designer Sport light (light worsted) weight yarn (3 oz/279 yds/85g per skein):
    7 skeins #3290 brick
- Size G/6/4mm crochet hook
- Size K/10½/6.5mm afghan hook or size needed to obtain gauge

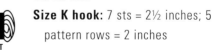

GAUGE

Size K hook: 7 sts = 2½ inches; 5 pattern rows = 2 inches

PATTERN NOTES

This item uses Stitch Pattern No. 2.
Join with slip stitch as indicated unless otherwise stated.

SPECIAL STITCHES

For step-by-step stitch information see Figs. 1–9 on pages 6–11.

Basic Foundation Row:

1. Work Loops On Hook (work lps on hook): Ch as stated, sk first ch, insert hook in 2nd ch from hook, yo, pull lp through ch, holding all lps on hook (you will now have 2 lps on hook), [insert hook in next ch, yo, pull lp through ch] across.

2. Standard Closing or Work Loops Off Hook (Standard Closing): Ch 1, [yo, pull through 2 lps on hook] across

Tunisian Reverse Stitch (TRS): Keeping hook to back of work, insert hook from right to left (side to side) under back vertical bar, yo, pull lp through.

Tunisian Knit Stitch (TKS): Insert hook from front to back of work, between front and back vertical bars of same st, yo, pull lp through.

INSTRUCTIONS

THROW

Row 1: Basic Foundation Row (see Special Stitches)

1. With size K hook, ch 146, **work lps on hook** (see Special Stitches);

2. Standard Closing (see Special Stitches). Last lp on hook counts as first st of next row.

Row 2:

1. Sk first vertical bar, **TRS** (see Special Stitches) across;

2. Standard Closing.

Row 3:

1. Ch 1, sk first vertical bar, *[yo, TRS] 5 times, 5 TRS, rep from * across to last 5 vertical bars, [yo, TRS] 5 times (221 lps on hook);

2. Ch 2, *[remove first lp from hook and drop yo from hook, replace first lp back on hook, yo, pull through 2 lps on hook] 5 times, [yo, pull through 2 lps on hook] 5 times, rep from * across to last 11 lps on hook, [remove next lp from hook, and drop yo from hook, replace lp back on hook, yo, pull through 2 lps on hook] 5 times.

Row 4:

1. Sk first vertical bar, TRS, [3 **TKS** (see Special Stitches), 7 TRS] across to last 4 vertical bars, 3 TKS, TRS in ch before last vertical bar;

2. Standard Closing.

Row 5: Rep row 2.

Row 6:

1. Sk first vertical bar, 5 TRS, *[yo, TRS] 5 times, 5 TRS, rep from * across (216 lps on hook);

2. Ch 1, *[yo, pull through 2 lps on hook] 5 times, [remove next lp from hook, drop yo from hook, replace lp back on hook, yo, pull through 2 lps on hook] 5 times, rep from * across to last 6 lps on hook, [yo, pull through 2 lps on hook] 5 times.

Row 7:

1. Sk first vertical bar, 6 TRS, [3 TKS, 7 TRS] across to last 9 vertical bars, 3 TKS, 6 TRS;

2. Standard Closing

Rows 8–127: [Rep rows 2–7 consecutively] 20 times.

Rows 128–130: Rep rows 2–4. At end of last row, **do not fasten off**.

TRIM

Rnd 1: Now working in rnds, with size G hook, ch 1, working as for TRS, 3 sc in first vertical bar, sc in each vertical bar across to last vertical bar, 3 sc in last vertical bar, evenly sp sc in ends of rows down side, working in starting ch on opposite side of row 1, 3 sc in first ch, sc in each ch across with 3 sc in last ch, evenly sp sc in ends of rows along side, **join** (see Pattern Notes) in beg sc.

Rnd 2: Working in **back lps** (see Stitch Guide), ch 1, sc in each st around with 3 sc in each center corner st, join in beg sc. Fasten off. ●

symphony capelet

SKILL LEVEL

INTERMEDIATE

FINISHED SIZE

One size fits most

MATERIALS

- Omega Sinfonia light (light worsted) weight yarn (3½ oz/218 yds/100g per skein):
   3 skeins #318 azul cenizo (denim)
- Size F/5/3.75mm crochet hook
- Size K/10½/6.5mm afghan hook or size needed to obtain gauge
- Sewing needle
- Sewing thread
- ½-inch round buttons: 3
- Stitch marker

GAUGE

Size K hook: 13 TKS = 4 inches; 14 pattern rows = 4 inches

PATTERN NOTE

This item uses Stitch Pattern No. 6.

SPECIAL STITCHES

For step-by-step stitch information see Figs. 1–9 on pages 6–11.

Basic Foundation Row:

Standard Closing or Work Loops Off Hook (Standard Closing): Ch 1, [yo, pull through 2 lps on hook] across

Tunisian Knit Stitch (TKS): Insert hook from front to back of work, between front and back vertical bars of same st, yo, pull lp through.

Tunisian Extended Stitch (TES): Insert hook from front to back, between front and back vertical bars of same st, yo, pull lp through, ch 1.

Make One (M1): Insert hook in ch-1 sp, yo, pull lp through.

Tunisian Knit Stitch decrease (TKS dec): Insert hook as for TKS through 2 vertical bars at same time, yo, pull lp through.

INSTRUCTIONS

CAPELET

Row 1:

1. Beg at bottom edge, with size K hook, ch 159, holding all lps on hook, insert hook in 2nd ch from hook, yo, pull lp through, insert hook in next ch, yo, pull lp through, *[insert hook in next ch, yo, pull lp through, ch 1] 3 times, [insert hook in next ch, yo, pull lp through] 3 times, rep from * across *(159 lps on hook)*;

2. Ch 1, [yo, pull through 2 lps on hook] twice, *ch 1, yo, pull through 4 lps on hook, ch 1, [yo, pull through 2 lps on hook] 3 times, rep from * across. Last lp on hook counts as first st of next row.

Row 2:

1. Sk first vertical bar, 2 **TKS** *(see Special Stitches)*, [insert hook in horizontal bar above next 3-st group, yo, pull lp through, 3 TKS] across *(107 lps on hook)*;

2. Ch 1, [yo, pull through 2 lps on hook] twice, *ch 1, yo, pull through 2 lps on hook, ch 1, [yo, pull through 2 lps on hook] 3 times, rep from * across.

Row 3:

1. Sk first vertical bar, 2 TKS, [**M1** *(see Special Stitches)*, ch 1, **TES** *(see Special Stitches)*, M1, ch 1, 3 TKS] across *(159 lps on hook)*;

2. Ch 1, [yo, pull through 2 lps on hook] twice, *ch 1, yo, pull through

Rows 35–37: [Rep row 27] 3 times.
Row 38:
1. Sk first vertical bar, TKS, [TKS dec, 5 TKS] across to last 4 vertical bars, TKS dec, 2 TKS *(71 lps on hook)*;
2. Standard Closing.
Rows 39–41: [Rep row 27] 3 times.
Row 42: With size F hook, ch 1, sk first vertical bar, sc as for TKS in each vertical bar across. Fasten off.

BOTTOM TRIM

With RS facing and size F hook, working in starting ch on opposite side of row 1, join with sl st in first ch, ch 2, hdc in each of next 2 chs, *[ch 1, dc in next ch] 3 times, ch 1, hdc in each of next 3 chs, rep from * across. Fasten off.

BUTTON BAND

Row 1: Working on left front, with RS facing and size F hook, join with sc in end of row 42, evenly sp sc down front to row 1, turn.
Rows 2 & 3: Ch 1, sc in each st across, turn. At end of last row, fasten off.

BUTTONHOLE BAND

Row 1: With RS facing and size F hook, join with sc in end of row 1, evenly sp sc across, turn.
Row 2: Mark 3 buttonholes at ¼-inch, 2½ inches and 4½ inches down from top edge, ch 1, *sc in each st across to first marker, [ch 1, sk next st], rep from * twice, sc in each st across, turn.
Row 3: Ch 1, sc in each st and in each ch across. Fasten off.
Sew buttons to Button Band opposite buttonholes. ●

4 lps on hook, ch 1, [yo, pull through 2 lps on hook] 3 times, rep from * across.
Rows 4–25: [Rep rows 2 and 3 alternately] 11 times.
Row 26:
1. Sk first vertical bar, 2 TKS, [insert hook in horizontal bar above next 3-st group, yo, pull lp through, 3 TKS] across *(107 lps on hook)*;
2. Standard Closing of Basic Foundation Row *(see Special Stitches)*.
Row 27:
1. Sk first vertical bar, TKS across;

2. Standard Closing
Rows 28 & 29: [Rep row 27] twice.
Row 30:
1. Sk first vertical bar, 2 TKS, [**TKS dec** *(see Special Stitches)*, 7 TKS] across to last 5 vertical bars, TKS dec, 3 TKS *(95 lps on hook)*;
2. Standard Closing.
Rows 31–33: Rep row 27.
Row 34:
1. Sk first vertical bar, 2 TKS, [TKS dec, 6 TKS] across to last 4 vertical bars, TKS dec, 2 TKS *(83 lps on hook)*;
2. Standard Closing.

carnival market bag

SKILL LEVEL

INTERMEDIATE

FINISHED SIZE

14 x 18 inches, excluding Handles

MATERIALS

- Red Heart Eco-Cotton Blend medium (worsted) weight yarn (3 oz/145 yds/85g per skein):

  4 MEDIUM

  3 skeins #1370 candy marl
- Size G/6/4mm crochet hook
- Size K/10½/6.5mm afghan hook or size needed to obtain gauge
- Stitch markers: 5

GAUGE

Size K hook: 5 cls = 3 inches;

PATTERN NOTES

This item uses Stitch Pattern No. 4.

Work in continuous rounds, do not turn or join unless otherwise stated.

Mark first stitch of each round.

Join with slip stitch as indicated unless otherwise stated.

SPECIAL STITCHES

For step-by-step stitch information see Figs. 1–9 on pages 6–11.

Basic Foundation Row:

Standard Closing or Work Loops Off Hook (Standard Closing): Ch 1, [yo, pull through 2 lps on hook] across

Tunisian Knit Stitch (TKS): Insert hook from front to back of work, between front and back vertical bars of same st, yo, pull lp through.

Tunisian Double Stitch (TDS): Yo, insert hook as for **TKS** or as indicated, yo, pull lp through, yo, pull through 2 lps on hook.

Tunisian Simple Stitch (TSS): Keeping hook in front of work, insert hook from right to left (side to side) under front vertical bar, yo, pull lp through.

Tunisian Treble Stitch (TTRS): Yo twice, insert hook as for **TKS** or as indicated, yo, pull lp through, [yo, pull through 2 lps on hook] twice.

Tunisian Cluster (TCL): Yo twice, insert hook as for **TSS** under 2 front vertical bars at same time, yo, pull lp through, [yo, pull through 2 lps on hook] twice, yo twice, insert hook under same 2 front vertical bars, yo, pull lp through, [yo, pull through 2 lps on hook] 3 times.

INSTRUCTIONS

BAG
BASE

Rnd 1: With size G hook, ch 46, 3 sc in 2nd ch from hook, sc in each of next 43 chs, 3 sc in last ch, working on opposite side of ch, sc in each of next 43 chs, **do not join** (see Pattern Notes). (92 sc)

Rnd 2: 3 sc in first st (mark center st), sc in next st, 3 sc in next st (mark center st), sc in each of next 43 sts, 3 sc in next st (mark center st), sc in corner st, 3 sc in next st (mark center st), sc in each of last 43 sts. (100 sc)

Rnd 3: Sc in each st around with 3 sc in each marked center st. (108 sc)

Rnd 4: Sc in each st around with 3 sc in each marked center st, **join** (see Pattern Notes) in beg sc, sl st in each of next 6 sts. **Do not fasten off**. (116 sc)

BODY
FIRST SIDE
Row 1:

1. Now working in rows, with size K hook, holding all lps on hook, ch 2, sk first sc, **TDS** (see Special Stitches) in each of next 57 sc, leaving rem sc unworked (58 lps on hook);

2. Standard Closing of Basic Foundation Row (see Special Stitches).

Row 2:
1. Ch 3, sk first vertical bar, **TCL** *(see Special Stitches)* across to last vertical bar, **TTRS** *(see Special Stitches)* in last vertical bar *(30 lps on hook)*;
2. [Ch 1, yo, pull through 2 lps on hook] across. ***Note:*** *This is not a Standard Closing.*
Row 3:
1. Ch 2, sk first vertical bar, [TDS by inserting hook under horizontal strand before TCL and ch-1 sp at same time, TDS as for TKS in cl] across to last vertical bar, TDS in top of TTRS *(58 lps on hook)*;
2. Standard Closing.
Rows 4–11: [Rep rows 2 and 3 alternately] 4 times. At end of last row, fasten off.

2ND SIDE
Rows 1–11: With RS facing and with size K hook, join in first unworked sc on rnd 4 of Base, rep rows 1–11 of First Side of Body.

SIDE SEAM
With size G hook, matching ends of rows on First and 2nd Sides, working around last st at ends of rows at same time, join with sl st, evenly sp sl st across. Fasten off.
Rep on rem side edges.

TOP
Rnd 1: With RS facing and size G hook, join at seam, ch 1, working in each vertical bar as for TKS, evenly sp 116 sc around, join in beg sc. *(116 sc)*
Rnd 2: Ch 1, sc in each of first 3 sts, sk next st, [sc in each of next 3 sts, sk next st] around, join in beg sc. *(87 sc)*
Rnd 3: Ch 1, sk first st, sc in each st around, join in beg sc. *(86 sc)*
Rnds 4–7: Ch 1, sc in each st around, join in beg sc.
Rnd 8: Ch 1, sc in each of first 5 sts, ch 50 *(Handle)*, sk next 33 sts, being careful not twist ch, sc in each of next 10 sts, ch 50 *(Handle)*, sk next 33 sts, being careful not to twist ch, sc in each of last 5 sts, join in beg sc.
Rnd 9: Ch 1, sc in each of first 5 sts, sc in each ch across, sc in each of next 10 sts, sc in each ch across, sc in each of last 5 sts, join in beg sc. *(120 sc)*
Rnd 10: Ch 1, sc in each st around, join in beg sc.
Rnd 11: Ch 3, sk next 8 sts, sc in each of next 43 sts, sk next 8 sts, tr in next st, sk next 8 sts, sc in each of next 43 sts, sk rem sts, join in 3rd ch of beg ch-3. **Do not fasten off.**

HANDLE JOINING
Holding Handles with WS tog, working through both thicknesses, ch 1, sl st in each of next 43 sts. Fasten off. ●

starburst

or join unless otherwise stated. Mark first stitch of each round.

SPECIAL STITCHES

For step-by-step stitch information see Figs. 1–9 on pages 6–11.

Basic Foundation Row:

1. Work Loops On Hook (work lps on hook): Ch as stated, sk first ch, insert hook in 2nd ch from hook, yo, pull lp through ch, holding all lps on hook (you will now have 2 lps on hook), [insert hook in next ch, yo, pull lp through ch] across.

2. Standard Closing or Work Loops Off Hook (Standard Closing): Ch 1, [yo, pull through 2 lps on hook] across.

Tunisian Knit Stitch (TKS): Insert hook from front to back of work, between front and back vertical bars of same st, yo, pull lp through.

Tunisian Double Stitch (TDS): Yo, insert hook as for **TKS** or as indicated, yo, pull lp through, yo, pull through 2 lps on hook.

Tunisian Reverse Stitch (TRS): Keeping hook to back of work, insert hook from right to left (side to side) under back vertical bar, yo, pull lp through.

Tunisian Knit Stitch decrease (TKS dec): Insert hook as for TKS through 2 vertical bars at same time, yo, pull lp through.

(see Special Stitches)

1. With size K hook, ch 35, **work lps on hook:** (see Special Stitches) (35 lps);

2. [Ch 2, yo, pull through 4 lps on hook] across to last 2 lps, ch 1, yo, pull though both lps on hook. Last lp on hook counts as first st of next row.

cloche & scarf

SKILL LEVEL

INTERMEDIATE

FINISHED SIZES

Scarf: 12 x 59½ inches
Hat: 23 inches circumference

MATERIALS

- Red Heart Designer Sport light (light worsted) weight yarn (3 oz/279 yds/85g per skein): 2 skeins #3601 cornsilk
- Sizes F/5/3.75mm and G/6/4mm crochet hooks
- Size K/10½/6.5mm afghan hook or size needed to obtain gauge
- Tapestry needle
- Large covered elastic ponytail bands: 2
- Stitch marker

GAUGE

Size K hook: 12 pattern sts = 3¾ inches; 4 pattern rows = 3 inches

PATTERN NOTES

This item uses Stitch Pattern No. 5.
Join with slip stitch as indicated unless otherwise stated.
Work in continuous rounds, do not turn

INSTRUCTIONS

SCARF

Row 1: Basic Foundation Row

Row 2:

1. Sk first vertical bar, [3 **TDS** (see Special Stitches) in horizontal bar above 3-st group] across to last vertical bar, **TKS** (see Special Stitches);

2. Standard Closing of Basic Foundation Row (see Special Stitches).

Row 3:

1. Sk first vertical bar, **TRS** (see Special Stitches) across to last vertical bar, TRS in ch before last vertical bar;

2. [Ch 2, yo, pull through 4 lps on hook] across to last 2 lps, ch 1, yo, pull though both lps on hook.

Rows 4–77: [Rep rows 2 and 3 alternately] 37 times.

Row 78:

1. Sk first vertical bar, [3 TDS in horizontal bar above 3-st group] across to last vertical bar, TKS;

2. Standard Closing.

Row 79: Sk first vertical bar, sl st as for TRS across. Fasten off.

TRIM

Rnd 1: Now working in rnds around outer edge in ends of rows and in sts, with size G hook, **join** (see Pattern Notes) in any corner, ch 1, 3 sc in same st *(corner)*, evenly sp sc around with 3 sc in each corner, join in beg sc.

Rnd 2: Working in **back lps** *(see Stitch Guide)*, ch 1, sc in each st around with 3 sc in each center corner st, join in beg sc. Fasten off.

SCARF CINCH

Rnd 1: Working around 1 ponytail band, with size G hook, join with sc **around band** *(see Fig. 1)*, 39 sc around, join in beg sc. *(40 sc)*

Fig. 1
Single Crochet around band.

Rnds 2–6: Ch 1, sc in each st around, join in beg sc. **Do not fasten off**.

Rnd 7: Working over rem ponytail band, ch 1, sc in each st around, join in beg sc. Fasten off.

STARBURST FLOWER

Rnd 1: With size F hook, ch 2, 6 sc in 2nd ch from hook, **do not join** *(see Pattern Notes)*. *(6 sc)*

Rnd 2: 2 sc in each st around. *(12 sc)*

Rnd 3: Sc in first st, [2 sc in next st, sc in next st] around to last st, 2 sc in last st. *(18 sc)*

Rnd 4: Sc in each of first 2 sts, [2 sc in next st, sc in each of next 2 sts] around to last st, 2 sc in last st, join in beg sc. *(24 sc)*

Rnd 5: *[Ch 7, sk next ch, sl st in next ch, sc in next ch, hdc in each of next 2 chs, dc in each of next 2 chs**, sk sc on last rnd, sl st in each of next 2 sc, rep from * around, ending last rep at **, sl st each of last 2 sts, join in joining sl st. Fasten off.

Sew Flower to Scarf Cinch as shown in photo.

CLOCHE

Row 1: Basic Foundation Row *(see Special Stitches)*

1. Beg at bottom, with size K hook, ch 74, work lps on hook. *(74 lps)*

Row 2:

1. Sk first vertical bar, **TKS** *(see Special Stitches)* across;

2. Standard Closing.

Rows 3 & 4: [Rep row 2] twice.

Row 5:

1. Sk first vertical bar, **TRS** *(see Special Stitches)* across;

2. [Ch 2, yo, pull through 4 lps on hook] across to last 2 lps on hook, ch 1, yo, pull through both lps on hook.

Row 6:

1. Sk first vertical bar, [3 **TDS** *(see Special Stitches)* in horizontal bar above 3-st group] across to last vertical bar, TKS;

2. Standard Closing.

Row 7:

1. Sk first vertical bar, TRS across to last vertical bar, TRS in ch before last vertical bar;

2. [Ch 2, yo, pull through 4 lps on hook] across to last 2 lps on hook, ch 1, yo, pull through both lps on hook.

Rows 8–11: [Rep rows 6 and 7 alternately] twice.

Row 12: Rep row 6.

Row 13:

1. Sk first vertical bar, TRS across to last vertical bar, TRS in ch before last vertical bar;

2. Standard Closing.

Row 14:

1. Sk first vertical bar, [4 TKS, **TKS dec** *(see Special Stitches)*] across to last vertical bar, TKS *(62 lps on hook)*;

2. Standard Closing.

Row 15:

1. Sk first vertical bar, [3 TKS, TKS dec] across to last vertical bar, TKS *(50 lps on hook)*;

2. Standard Closing.

Row 16:

1. Sk first vertical bar, [2 TKS, TKS dec] across to last vertical bar, TKS *(38 lps on hook)*;

2. Standard Closing.

Row 17:

1. Sk first vertical bar, [TKS, TKS dec] across to last vertical bar, TKS *(26 lps on hook)*;

2. Standard Closing.

Row 18:

1. Sk first vertical bar, [TKS dec] across to last vertical bar, TKS *(14 lps on hook)*;

2. Standard Closing.

Row 19:

1. Sk first vertical bar, [TKS dec] across to last vertical bar, TKS *(8 lps on hook)*;

2. Standard Closing.

Row 20: Sk first vertical bar, [TKS dec] across to last vertical bar, TKS *(5 lps on hook)*, leaving 20-inch end, fasten off.

FINISHING

Weave 20-inch end through 5 lps on hook, pull to close.

Using same end, with WS facing, matching ends of rows, working around last st at ends of rows at same time, sew across for seam. Fasten off.

FLOWER

Work same as Starburst Flower for Scarf. Sew Flower to Hat as shown in photo. ●

rolled collar wrap

SKILL LEVEL

INTERMEDIATE

FINISHED SIZE

15¾ x 67 inches

MATERIALS

- Omega Passy light (light worsted) weight yarn (1¾ oz/186 yds/50g per skein):
    3 balls #984 verde
- Size F/5/3.75mm crochet hook
- Size K/10½/6.5mm afghan hook or size needed to obtain gauge

GAUGE

Size K hook: 12 pattern sts = 4 inches; 6 pattern rows = 4 inches unblocked

PATTERN NOTE

This item uses Stitch Pattern No. 9.

SPECIAL STITCHES

For step-by-step stitch information see Figs. 1–9 on pages 6–11.

Basic Foundation Row:

1. **Work Loops On Hook (work lps on hook):** Ch as stated, sk first ch, insert hook in 2nd ch from hook, yo, pull lp through ch, holding all lps on hook (you will now have 2 lps on hook), [insert hook in next ch, yo, pull lp through ch] across.

2. **Standard Closing or Work Loops Off Hook (Standard Closing):** Ch 1, [yo, pull through 2 lps on hook] across.

Tunisian Simple Stitch (TSS): Keeping hook to front of work, insert hook from right to left (side to side) under front vertical bar, yo, pull lp through.

Tunisian Knit Stitch (TKS): Insert hook from front to back of work, between front and back vertical bars of same st, yo, pull lp through.

Tunisian Double Stitch (TDS): Yo, insert hook as for **TKS** or as indicated, yo, pull lp through, yo, pull through 2 lps on hook.

Make One (M1): Insert hook in ch-1 sp, yo, pull lp through.

Tunisian Knit Stitch decrease (TKS dec): Insert hook as for TKS through 2 vertical bars at same time, yo, pull lp through.

Tunisian Simple Stitch decrease (TSS dec): Insert hook as for TSS through 2 vertical bars at same time, yo, pull lp through.

INSTRUCTIONS

SHAWL

Row 1: Basic Foundation Row *(see Special Stitches)*

1. With size K hook, ch 200, **work lps on hook** *(see Special Stitches)* *(200 lps)*;

2. **Standard Closing** *(see Special Stitches).*

Row 2:

1. Ch 1, sk first 3 vertical bars, **TDS** *(see Special Stitches)* in next vertical bar, working in front of last TDS, TDS in 2nd sk vertical bar, [sk next 2 vertical bars, TDS in next vertical bar, TDS in first sk vertical bar] across to last vertical bar, TDS as for TKS in last vertical bar *(134 lps on hook)*;

2. Ch 1, [yo, pull through 2 lps on hook] 4 times, [yo, pull through 2 lps on hook, ch 1, yo, pull through 2 lps on hook] across to last 6 lps on hook, [yo, pull through 2 lps on hook] 5 times.

Row 3:
1. Sk first vertical bar, **TSS dec** *(see Special Stitches)*, 2 **TSS** *(see Special Stitches)*, [TSS, **M1** *(see Special Stitches)*, TSS] across to last 5 vertical bars, 2 TSS, TSS dec, TSS *(194 lps on hook)*;
2. Standard Closing.

Rows 4–21: [Rep rows 2 and 3 alternately] 9 times. *(140 lps on last row)*

Row 22:
1. Sk first vertical bar, **TKS dec** *(see Special Stitches)*, TKS across to last 3 vertical bars, TKS dec, TKS *(138 lps on hook)*;
2. Standard Closing.

Rows 23–25: [Rep row 2] 3 times.

Row 26: Sk first vertical bar, [sl st as for TKS dec] 5 times, sl st as for TKS across to last 10 vertical bars, [sl st as for TKS dec] 5 times. Fasten off.

TRIM
Row 1:
1. Working in starting ch on opposite side of row 1, join with sl st in first ch, ch 1, insert hook in next ch, yo, pull lp through, [insert hook in next ch, yo, pull lp through] across *(200 lps on hook)*;
2. Ch 1, [yo, pull through 4 lps on hook, ch 3] across to last 5 lps on hook, yo, pull through 4 lps on hook, yo, pull through 2 lps on hook.

Row 2:
1. Ch 2, [insert hook in ch-3 sp, yo, pull lp through] across to last vertical bar, TDS in last vertical bar;
2. Ch 1, yo, pull through 2 lps on hook, [ch 2, yo, pull through 2 lps on hook] across.

Row 3: With size F hook, ch 2, [5 dc in next ch-2 sp, sc in next ch-2 sp] across to last vertical bar, dc as for TKS. Fasten off. ●

swirls
baby afghan

swirls baby afghan

SKILL LEVEL

■■■□ **INTERMEDIATE**

FINISHED SIZE

41 inches in diameter

MATERIALS

- Red Heart Designer Sport light (light worsted) weight yarn (3 oz/ 279 yds/85g per skein):
  - 3 skeins #3620 celadon
  - 1 skein each #3101 ivory and #3601 cornsilk
- Size G/6/4mm crochet hook
- Size K/10½/6.5mm afghan hook or size needed to obtain gauge
- Tapestry needle

GAUGE

Size K hook: 1 pattern sts = 1 inch

PATTERN NOTES

This item uses Stitch Pattern No. 10.

Each row is worked in 2 parts.

Join with slip stitch as indicated unless otherwise stated.

Chain-3 at beginning of row or round counts as first double crochet unless otherwise stated.

Chain-5 at beginning of row or round counts as first double crochet and chain-2 unless otherwise stated.

SPECIAL STITCHES

For step-by-step stitch information see Figs. 1–9 on pages 6–11.

Basic Foundation Row:

1. Work Loops On Hook (work lps on hook): Ch as stated, sk first ch, insert hook in 2nd ch from hook, yo, pull lp through ch, holding all lps on hook (you will now have 2 lps on hook), [insert hook in next ch, yo, pull lp through ch] across.

2. Standard Closing or Work Loops Off Hook (Standard Closing): Ch 1, [yo, pull through 2 lps on hook] across

Tunisian Knit Stitch (TKS): Insert hook from front to back of work, between front and back vertical bars of same st, yo, pull lp through.

V-stitch (V-st): (Dc, ch 2, dc) in place indicated.

INSTRUCTIONS

AFGHAN

Row 1: Basic Foundation Row (see Special Stitches)

1. With size K hook and celadon, ch 53, **work lps on hook** (see Special Stitches) (53 lps on hook);

2. [Ch 2, yo, pull through 4 lps on hook] across to last 2 lps on hook, ch 1, yo, pull through both lps on hook. Last lp on hook counts as first st of next row.

Row 2:

1. Sk first vertical bar, insert hook in horizontal bar above next 3-st group, yo, pull lp through, yo, insert hook in same horizontal bar, yo, pull lp through, [insert hook in horizontal bar above next 3-st group, yo, pull lp through, yo, insert hook in same horizontal bar, yo, pull lp through] across to last ch-2 sp before horizontal bar above last 3-st group, insert hook

in ch-2 sp, yo, pull lp through (50 lps on hook);

2. Standard Closing of Basic Foundation Row (see Special Stitches).

Row 3:

1. Sk first vertical bar, **TKS** (see Special Stitches) across to last 3 vertical bars, leaving last 3 bars unworked (47 lps on hook);

2. [Ch 2, yo, pull through 4 lps on hook] across to last 2 lps on hook, ch 1, yo, pull through both lps on hook.

Rows 4–17: [Rep rows 2 and 3 alternately] 7 times. (5 lps on last row)

Row 18:

1. Sk first vertical bar, insert hook in horizontal bar above first 3-st group, yo, pull lp through, yo, insert hook in same horizontal bar, yo, pull lp through, TKS in last vertical bar of row, [TKS in 3 unworked vertical bars on row below, insert hook in unused horizontal bar above 3-st group of next row below, yo, pull lp through, yo, TKS in last vertical bar of row] across all rows (53 lps on hook);

2. Place slip knot with ivory on hook, [ch 2, yo, pull through 4 lps on hook] across to last 2 lps on hook, ch 1, yo, pull through both lps on hook. Fasten off celadon.

Rows 19–34: With ivory, rep rows 2–17.

Row 35:

1. Sk first vertical bar, insert hook in horizontal bar above first 3-st group, yo, pull lp through, yo, insert hook in same horizontal bar, yo, pull lp through, TKS in last vertical bar of row, [TKS in 3 unworked vertical bars

on row below, insert hook in unused horizontal bar above 3-st group of next row below, yo, pull lp through, yo, TKS in last vertical bar of row] across all rows *(53 lps on hook)*;

2. Place slip knot with celadon on hook, [ch 2, yo, pull through 4 lps on hook] across to last 2 lps on hook, ch 1, yo, pull through both lps on hook. Fasten off ivory.

Rows 36–188: Working in color sequence of celadon, cornsilk, celadon and ivory, [rep rows 19–35 consecutively] 9 times. *(11 wedges completed)*

Rows 189–204: With cornsilk, rep 1 and 2 of rows 19–34.

Row 205:

1. Sk first vertical bar, insert hook in horizontal bar above first 3-st group, yo, pull lp through, yo, insert hook in same horizontal bar, yo, pull lp through, TKS in last vertical bar of row, [TKS in 3 unworked vertical bars on row below, insert hook in unused horizontal bar above 3-st group of next row below, yo, pull lp through, yo, TKS in last vertical bar of row] across all rows *(53 lps on hook)*;

2. Place slip knot with celadon on hook, [ch 2, yo, pull through 4 lps on hook] across to last 2 lps on hook, ch 1, yo, pull through both lps on hook. Leaving 20-inch end of celadon, fasten off all colors.

FINISHING

Using tapestry needle and 20-inch end, sew first and last rows tog, weave end through ends of rows at center, pull to close. Secure end.

TRIM

Rnd 1: With size G hook, **join** *(see Pattern Notes)* celadon in end of any row, **ch 3** *(see Pattern Notes)*, dc in same row, 2 dc in end of each row around, join in 3rd ch of beg ch-3. *(410 dc)*

Rnd 2: Ch 5 *(see Pattern Notes)*, dc in same st, [sk next dc, sc in next dc, ch 3, sc in next dc, sk next dc, **V-st** *(see Special Stitches)* in next dc] around to last 4 dc, sk next dc, sc in next dc, ch 3, sc in next dc, sk last dc, join in 3rd ch of beg ch-5.

Rnd 3: Sl st in first ch sp, ch 3, 4 dc in same ch sp, [ch 3, sk next ch sp, 5 dc in ch sp of next V-st] around, ch 3, join in 3rd ch of beg ch-3.

Rnd 4: Ch 5, dc in same st, [sk next st, V-st in next st] twice, *working over ch-3 sps of last 2 rnds tog, sc in next ch sp on rnd before last**, V-st in next dc, [sk next dc, V-st in next dc] twice, rep from * around, ending last rep at **, join in 3rd ch of beg ch-3.

Rnd 5: Sl st in first ch sp, ch 1, sc in same ch sp, *ch 2, V-st in ch sp of next V-st, ch 2**, sc in ch sp of each of next 2 V-sts, rep from * around, ending last rep at **, sc in ch sp of last V-st, join in beg sc.

Rnd 6: Sl st in first ch sp, ch 1, 2 sc in same ch sp, *ch 1, (tr, ch 1) 5 times in ch sp of next V-st**, 2 sc in each of next 2 ch sps, rep from * around, ending last rep at **, 2 sc in last ch sp, join in beg sc. Fasten off. ●

opulent

shells wrap

SKILL LEVEL

INTERMEDIATE

FINISHED SIZE
24 x 70 inches unblocked, excluding trim

MATERIALS
- Drops Vivaldi medium (worsted) weight yarn (1¾ oz/306 yds/50g per skein): 3 balls #16 rust
- Size G/6/4mm crochet hook
- Size K/10½/6.5mm afghan hook or size needed to obtain gauge

GAUGE
Size K hook: 5 sts = 2¾ inches; 5 pattern rows = 6½ inches unblocked

PATTERN NOTES
This item uses Stitch Pattern No. 7.

Wrap is made beginning at center back, working in one direction, with a cast on and picking up stitches to work in opposite direction.

Join with slip stitch as indicated unless otherwise stated.

SPECIAL STITCHES
For step-by-step stitch information see Figs. 1–9 on pages 6–11.

Tunisian Knit Stitch (TKS): Insert hook from front to back of work, between front and back vertical bars of same st, yo, pull lp through.

Tunisian Treble Stitch (TTRS): Yo twice, insert hook as for **TKS** or as indicated, yo, pull lp through, [yo, pull through 2 lps on hook] twice.

Tunisian Double Stitch (TDS): Yo, insert hook as for **TKS** or as indicated, yo, pull lp through, yo, pull through 2 lps on hook.

INSTRUCTIONS

WRAP
FIRST SIDE
Row 1:

1. Ch 93, holding all lps on hook, yo twice, insert hook in 3rd ch from hook, [yo, pull through 2 lps on hook] twice, *sk next 4 chs, [yo, insert hook in next ch, yo, pull lp through, yo, pull through 2 lps on hook] 5 times, sk next 4 chs, **yo twice, insert hook in next ch, yo, pull lp through, [yo, pull through 2 lps on hook] twice, rep from ** once, rep from * across (44 lps on hook);

2. Ch 1, [yo, pull through 2 lps on hook] twice, *[ch 1, yo, pull through 2 lps on hook] 4 times, [yo, pull through 2 lps on hook] 3 times, rep from * across to last 7 lps on hook, [ch 1, yo, pull through 2 lps on hook] 4 times, [yo, pull though 2 lps on hook] twice.

Row 2:

1. Ch 2, sk first vertical bar, **TTRS** (see Special Stitches) as for **TKS** (see Special Stitches) in next vertical bar, [5 **TDS** (see Special Stitches) as for TKS in 3rd st of next 5-st group, TTRS as for TKS in each of next 2 TTRS] across;

2. Ch 1, [yo, pull through 2 lps on hook] twice, *[ch 1, yo, pull through 2 lps on hook] 4 times, [yo, pull through 2 lps on hook] 3 times, rep from * across to last 7 lps on hook, [ch 1, yo, pull through 2 lps on hook] 4 times, [yo, pull though 2 lps on hook] twice.

Rows 3–27: Rep row 2. At end of last row, **do not fasten off**.

opulent shells wrap

TRIM

With size G hook, working as for TKS, sk first vertical bar, sl st in each of next 3 vertical bars, sl st in next vertical bar, *ch 30, sl st in same vertical bar, ch 40, sl st in same vertical bar, ch 30, sl st in same vertical bar**, sl st in each of next 6 vertical bars, rep from * across, ending last rep at **, sl st in each of last 4 vertical bars. Fasten off.

2ND SIDE

Row 1:

1. Working in starting ch on opposite side of row 1 and with size K hook, join with sl st in first ch, ch 2, TTRS in next ch, [sk next 4 chs, TDS in each of next 5 chs, sk next 4 chs, TTRS in each of next 2 chs] across *(44 lps on hook)*;

2. Ch 1, [yo, pull through 2 lps on hook] twice, *[ch 1, yo, pull through 2 lps on hook] 4 times, [yo, pull through

56 LEARN TO DO TUNISIAN LACE STITCH • Annie's Attic • Berne, IN 46711 • AnniesAttic.com